First published 2016.

This book was co-written and designed with Write Business Results, who provide book packages to entrepreneurs. Write Business Results partner with Scarletta Design.

This book is authored by Graeme Hall, and all intellectual property within belongs to Graeme Hall. All rights are reserved. If you would like to quote a sentence or concept from this book, then Graeme Hall, Sales Blueprint and this book's title must be properly referenced. For a longer segment of text, or to use any of Graeme Hall's intellectual property, you must obtain his permission in writing.

salesblueprint

Contents

Introduction — 4

1 Building A Scalable & Sustainable Sales Operation — 9
The 3 Cs Methodology
1.1 Characterise — 10
1.2 Capacity — 22
1.3 Conduct — 32

2 The Keys To Maintenance & Continuous Improvement — 41
Sales Management Skills & Processes
2.1 The Role Of Sales Management — 42
2.2 Succession Planning — 55
2.3 Key Account Planning — 58

3 The Secrets To Outperforming The Plan — 62
Importance of a High Performing Culture
3.1 Creating a High Performing Culture — 63
3.2 Setting Targets for a High Performing Culture — 70
3.3 Working Together for a High Performing Culture — 74
3.4 High-Performance Meetings & Field Visits — 78

4 If You Can't Change The People, Change The People — 81
Human Capital
4.1 Getting The Right Talent — 82
4.2 An Induction Process For Faster Performance — 88
4.3 Summary — 92

Appendices — 97

Introduction

When private equity began around 30 years ago, in simple terms, potential investors used to simply look at the financials of a company, do some management interviews, work to the business plan, and it either worked or it didn't. Over the last two decades, an ever-increasing variety of due diligence has been employed to minimise risk, take some of that uncertainty out of the process, and improve financial results.

Rather than just trusting their judgment, the majority of private equity firms might get an independent assessment of how successful the business leadership team are and how effectively their teams work together, what the dynamics might be, and how it might be possible to make things work better. But until we came up with the idea of sales operations due diligence (thanks in no small part to a sadly deceased chap from the private equity community in Birmingham called Harry Fellows) and packaged it in a robust process, nobody was doing it. It simply wasn't a thing.

To us, and quite a few others now we're pleased to say, it makes perfect sense. Most mid-market private equity firms back businesses on the basis of growing the top line in order to grow the bottom line. The less risk an investor perceives in that transaction, the higher potential value there is in the investment and the company will sit at a higher multiple (or, in the case of a sale by private equity, a multiple of a higher number). So it's not surprising that more and more private equity firms are now making optimising sales operations an important part of their model. They are starting to recognize the significant value of our operational expertise more than they might have done previously.

I set up my company, Sales Blueprint, in response to the recognition that many companies are failing to fulfill their growth potential due to inefficient or ineffective sales processes. I've been very fortunate in my career to have been exposed to some amazing people with excellent processes, but it became clear to me that this is the exception, not the rule. Most companies only know what they already know, and can't see where the improvement potential lies or how to change. Most SMEs simply don't know what 'good' looks like.

Unlike other aspects of business, such as marketing, administration and management, there is no formal standard or qualification for sales leaders. No-one can get a degree in Sales Operations and as a result, leaders and Sales Managers are left to try their hardest and hope for the best. After years of working with private equity invested companies, coaching them on best sales operations practice and helping them to multiply the effectiveness of their salespeople, improve management practices and become significantly more profitable, I've developed a unique methodology and process that I'm about to share with you in this book.

Our Three 'C' methodology

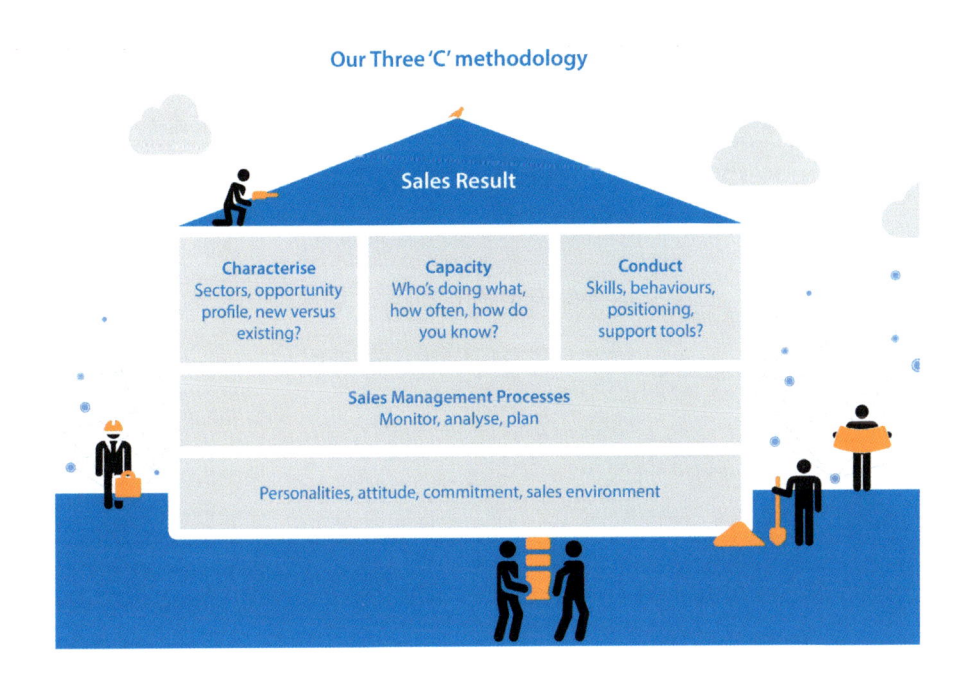

Sales Result

Characterise	Capacity	Conduct
Sectors, opportunity profile, new versus existing?	Who's doing what, how often, how do you know?	Skills, behaviours, positioning, support tools?

Sales Management Processes
Monitor, analyse, plan

Personalities, attitude, commitment, sales environment

We call this The 3 Cs Model and this book will take you through each of the component parts, explaining what "good" looks like, and how you can achieve it in your business.

Written for Operational Partners, Industrial Partners, and above all General Partners seeking to understand how they can go from doing well to experiencing growth in situations where things had previously stalled, this book is your best practice guide and is designed to be read in as little as 90 minutes. By the end of it you will understand our 3 Cs Methodology, the keys to successful sales management, including how to find the right talent, and how to manage your human capital.

You'll find it's particularly useful to read just before you go in to look at a potential investment (especially the 'tips to avoid the traps' questions at the end of each chapter), or perhaps to refresh your memory prior to attending a board meeting at a company that might not be hitting their top line.

Because of the experience we have had over the years, working at all levels in the sales department, we have been there and done it. We've made all the mistakes that teach the best lessons, and learnt from some very skilled Sales Managers and theorists. We have a particularly strong and rather rare perspective on what best practice looks like in sales operations. This is critical, because whatever type of strategy you're devising, you can't get where you want to be if you don't know what your destination looks like.

The big question this book answers therefore, and the one we're asked all the time by private equity firms, is "What does 'good' look like?" Our expertise, experience and belief in a rigorous process of sales operations evaluation and improvement, and our approach to replacing subjective judgements with objective benchmarks, allows us to answer that question categorically.

1

Building A Scalable & Sustainable Sales Operation

The 3 Cs Methodology

Overview

1.1 Characterise

1.2 Capacity

1.3 Conduct

Our Three 'C' methodology

Characterise	Capacity	Conduct
Sectors, opportunity profile, new versus existing?	Who's doing what, how often, how do you know?	Skills, behaviours, positioning, support tools?

Sales Management Processes
Monitor, analyse, plan

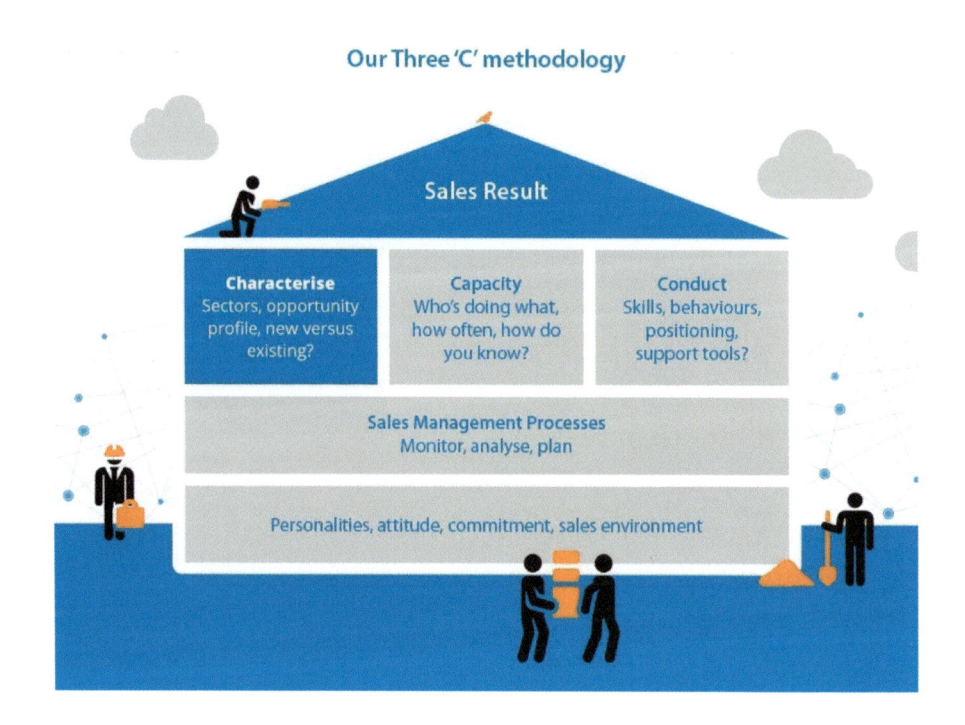

Personalities, attitude, commitment, sales environment

1.1 Characterise

Characterise	Capacity	Conduct
Sectors, opportunity profile, new versus existing?	Who's doing what, how often, how do you know?	Skills, behaviours, positioning, support tools?

When it comes to sales operations, there's no agreed best practice model. There is no go-to reference book. There are no formal qualifications. There may be many publications out there - for example, at the time of writing there are 66,109 results returned for 'sales management' on Amazon.co.uk – but there's actually no definitive guide, particularly for the unique demands of private equity-backed businesses. Until now.

There are lots of self-professed experts making money out of being able to tell people how to sell better, and I'm not saying they're all wrong, but many of them focus on what I call 'transactional' selling. In other words 'short-term' or 'one-hit' selling. There's no client relationship required, after-sales satisfaction may be low, and it's not a sustainable way of going about filling an order book. That's part of what gets sales a bad name.

Professional selling is actually still pretty rare in the UK. The best examples of this sort of strategy in action can be found in the IT industry, most often among US-based firms. Our model for making that work is simpler than you might expect. You just have to get three things right, and then keep them that way via proper sales management processes of course!

We call it our 3 Cs Methodology, and it all centres around Characterise, Capacity and Conduct. The first C stands for 'Characterise'.

It's important to identify the type of business that you want to win. Whether this task is assigned to the MD, the CEO, or possibly the Sales Director, it certainly needs to be decided by senior management. The risk is, if nobody specifies this focus, the salespeople will make their own choices.

Firstly, this is a problem because it's likely that each member of the sales force will identify the type of business they personally like to court, rather than the type of business that will benefit the organisation's overall goals. Here you risk short-termism, because many salespeople will choose easy wins not usually associated with the long game, and miss valuable cross-sell and upsell opportunities. Secondly, chances are every salesperson will come up with a different answer so there's no consistency. Thirdly, it's less likely that the target business will align with what the shareholders want for the long-term value of the business.

Characterisation is also about identifying the sort of resource you need to deliver the required results. The board therefore needs to decide on things such as how much brand new business they want, compared to the existing situation. Most businesses don't consider that at all. They just say, "We want 10% growth," and that's just not a detailed enough aim to be able to plan an effective sales strategy. It matters because the skills to deliver those things are different. You might want a team of hunters, and/or a team of farmers.

We have seen businesses decide that they are going to have some people that are going to hunt and farm. It rarely works. We accept that sometimes the size of the sales force that the business can afford dictates that people have to do both, but such a situation has to be very carefully managed if is to succeed. For most of the time you either hunt, or you farm. You can't do both well. It takes a different personality.

Some people, and I am one of them, like new things. Whenever we get a new enquiry, it's always more interesting than what I've had for a while. Even if the one I've had is worth six figures, the new one worth five figures is interesting. So I'm not the best member of our team when it comes to farming. Farmers say, "I've got this already, I'm not interested in the thrill of the chase, I'm interested in developing long-term relationships, looking for opportunities, and I might spend a year developing a proposition that works for them." These are two different sets of people and there is no one salesperson, that we have come across, that successfully does both all of the time.

There are a number of more detailed questions that need to be answered in order to be clear about the sort of business that will need to be generated:

- How much growth do we want?
- Which markets do we want to be in?
- Which markets are we definitely not going to be in?
- Will growth be built on existing products and services or a new proposition?
- What will the pricing architecture be?
- What are the margin expectations?
- Are we selling direct, or through partners?
- If selling through partners, what's the split percentage-wise?

With the answers to these questions, the sales management team can build the right opportunity profile to fulfil the set objectives. For example, if a Sales Director is told that their aim is to achieve 20% new logo business and 80% existing business over the following year, they will be able to consider all the company's major clients and, with a proper account planning process, ascertain the opportunities and timescales involved in order to build an approximation of how that 80% might be delivered. They can then plan the resource and activity necessary to deliver the 20% new business accordingly.

It's worth saying that there's no right answer when it comes to the split between new clients and repeat business. Even if the business management team isn't quite sure what the target percentages might be, setting clear objectives is more important than prevaricating over the exact figures – the sales management team don't know either, so it's better to make the decision and tell them, or they simply won't be able to deliver to your expectations.

As soon as the Sales Director knows the numbers, they can start to plan in detail how those numbers might be achieved, and ask themselves the pertinent questions that will help them to pin down the most effective resource and process to deliver the necessary sales (in terms of appropriate skill set, process, marketing support, opportunities and prospect evaluation). Ultimately, he or she will need to ascertain which clients (new or existing) are worth spending time and effort on to deliver the growth.

When you consider that the biggest cost of sale is typically the time and effort that you put into the business that you don't win, this narrowing of focus to identify and pursue the right sales opportunities is the only sensible way to operate. If you ask most salespeople about their success ratio, most of them won't know. If you ask them to guess, chances are they'll say one in three. Everyone says one in three, because that sounds about right. But if you flip that around, what they're really saying is that approximately two-thirds of their effort is wasted. How many jobs are there where you can waste two-thirds of your effort and still be a success? Not many.

To be fair, some of the 'wasted' effort is in fact about building a pipeline for the following year, so two-thirds isn't quite an accurate figure, but even if you adjusted the estimate to half, with a conversion rate of say one in two, that's still a waste of half an employee's time. At the end of the day, if you can direct their sales efforts more accurately, you have a chance of reducing that wasted time effort. That's why it's so important to profile the right opportunities, which is only possible when you have set objectives coming down from the business management team.

When it comes to focussing sales activity on the best opportunities (as you define them), it's important to have a solid process to evaluate each potential target, since not all are equal. So what are the characteristics of the right opportunity? They might come down to simple things, like businesses of a particular turnover, with a certain number of people, with a minimum number of locations. An evaluation will likely begin with such tangible things, but more subjective aspects might come into play, especially further along in the process once you've had an initial meeting. For example, if you're selling outsourced services, what is the target company's attitude to outside help? If they are the sort of organization to keep things in house, your proposition could be utterly brilliant, but it's still not likely to go far.

As well as considering subjective factors that might not be apparent until you actually engage with a target company, there is also the issue of competition affecting the viability of an opportunity. Competitors will likely either already be selling to that company, or perhaps just courting them. A good Sales Manager will be able to identify which competitors can be easily beaten, and which represent more of a challenge.

You might say the opportunity profile for each target is in two parts. If boxes are ticked within the first part, then the business is desirable, and if boxes are ticked within the second part, then it's likely that the business will be won. The second part here is key. Not only should each prospect be weighed up to decide whether they represent the sort of business that is desirable, but also whether it's achievable (rather than simply aspirational) and therefore whether it's worthwhile spending the necessary time and effort in order to pursue a sale[1].

Case Study: Characterise

We worked with a sizable IT provider, some years ago, who provided the most extreme example of what can happen if management is not definitive at the Characterise stage of its thinking.

---

[1] See appendix [Ideal Opportunity Profile]

Our efforts were part of an investigation into why sales were 20% behind plan despite the best product offer in the industry and an aggressive pricing plan.

What we found was:
- Over half of the 100-strong sales force were earning around £120k though they were on a £25k basic
- Cross-selling and up-selling were almost non-existent
- Of the 64 product lines available to be sold, 85% of sales were for two of them. These produced the lowest margins and the least 'sticky' customers

When things came to a head and the investors/lenders refused to provide any more money without radical change (this was not a private equity deal in the normal sense), the new management team took an axe to the customer base and 'sacked' a third of them on the basis that they were more expensive to service than the revenue (let alone margin) that they delivered.

Management's new plan resulted in a greatly reduced company, albeit one that was now solvent, which was subsequently sold, returning little real value for the original shareholders.

What caused this wasn't just that the commission scheme was too simplistic in rewarding all types of business equally - so unsurprisingly the sales force sold where it was quick, easy and comfortable - more that the ideal opportunity was neither defined nor measured, and the sales targets were set as one number alone.

Time spent thinking carefully about the size and shape of the desired growth, before embarking on the activity to deliver it, would have yielded proper segmentation of where the business needed to be won from, and unambiguous clarification of the various types of customer required to satisfy sustainable growth plans.

This could then have been supported by a compensation plan that rewarded the behaviour necessary to sell in this way. It would also have necessitated a much deeper understanding of the margins associated with each product line, before they went to market, and also what type of prospective customer might have valued each enough to perhaps pay a higher price for it.
 In the end, the only (short-term) winners were the sales force, who had a very easy ride for a couple of years before moving on to the next gravy train!

ⓘ TIPS TO AVOID THE TRAPS

- Why were the market sectors chosen and what are the anticipated revenues per sector? How do you know?
- Can you describe the 'ideal' opportunity? Is this information used to qualify new opportunities? If these criteria were applied to the current pipeline, how much of it would pass muster?
- How many of today's sales force could describe the ideal opportunity in the same way? Do new starts get access to this information currently?
- Has the planned growth been identified from new or existing accounts? Is this split reflected in the targets given to the sales force?
- Are the sales force being asked to hunt and farm, and how are the different skills associated with each acquired?

Our Three 'C' methodology

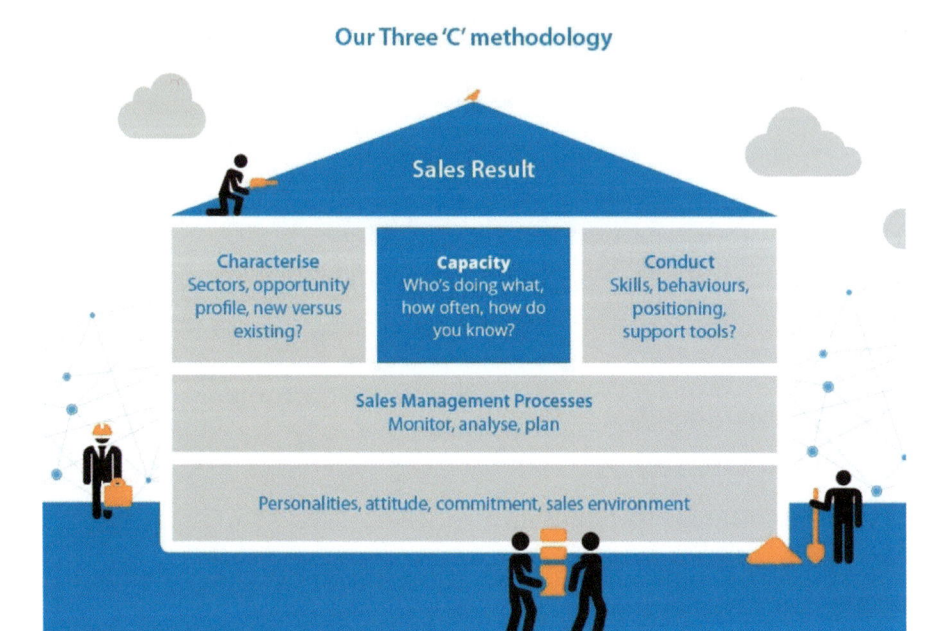

Characterise	Capacity	Conduct
Sectors, opportunity profile, new versus existing?	Who's doing what, how often, how do you know?	Skills, behaviours, positioning, support tools?

Sales Result

Sales Management Processes
Monitor, analyse, plan

Personalities, attitude, commitment, sales environment

1.2 Capacity

Characterise	Capacity	Conduct
Sectors, opportunity profile, new versus existing?	Who's doing what, how often, how do you know?	Skills, behaviours, positioning, support tools?

I'm always amazed how common it is for organisations to not know their sales capacity. For example, if a company builds laptops, and the MD goes to the Operations Director on the third Friday afternoon of the month and says, "Okay, we've got this order for 1,000 laptops. Can we ship them by the end of the month?" The Operations Director could give one of two answers. They could say, "Yes, I don't see why not, we have done it before, let's give it a go." How would the MD feel do you think?

However, if the Operations Director were able to give a much better informed answer, the MD's confidence level would be completely different. What they would want to hear is perhaps something like, "Well, I know how many motherboards I've got, I know how many screens I've got, how many keyboards I've got, and how many bodies I've got. Then 1,000 batteries are coming in on Monday, so we should have all the components.

I know how long it takes to build each one, I know what the capacity within each of my assembly processes is. I know I can process a certain number each day. I know what the total of man hours is for a week. I've put all that into a spreadsheet, and it spits out the fact that we could ship 500 in that time. However, I also know my scrap rate, which is 1%. Actually, we've got 500 in stock already, so I reckon we could fulfil that order within a week."

Often a Sales Director is asked for a projection, usually based on what customers have spent in the previous year, with a percentage added on top to fulfil the growth that's expected.

They are then then asked by the MD to confirm whether those figures are achievable based on the available budget. More often than not they'll simply say, "Yeah, why not, we can give it a go." Then they will cascade that into sales force targets, all slightly bigger than the previous year, so that everybody has got the message about growth and they're all thinking, "It's a bit of a stretch, but we will give it a go."

Now, you wouldn't accept that level of woolliness about any other aspect of the business. For example, there would be shock if the FD didn't pin their numbers down properly, so why should sales be any different? At the end of the day, when a projection isn't met, many questions will be asked. But since the original promise wasn't based on definitive knowledge, it's impossible to figure out exactly why the target wasn't hit, and those questions often can't be answered.

Our approach is to say, "Why wouldn't a Sales Director work out their sales process just as clearly as a manufacturer of laptops might pin down the manufacturing process, so it's easy to tell what's achievable in terms of capacity?" Best practice is to figure out the leanest route from one end of the sales process to the other. We get a lead, we qualify it, but then what do we do? Normally, we would telephone the potential customer, go and meet them to understand a bit more about what they want, put together a proposal, do a final negotiation, take the proposal back, present it to them, and finally they make a buying decision.

Of course, it's necessary to be flexible. Sometimes clients simply won't let a company stick to the usual order of things if they've got a procurement process that is conflicting. Generally speaking in most companies though, most of the business can be done according to an agreed process. Once the sales process and its dependencies have been set, you can map out (using a guesstimate, if necessary) the length of time each step takes, and work out how long it might take to deliver an agreed amount of business based on all the sales process activities and the conversion ratios.

To achieve a genuine figure it's important to only count available selling time, so by excluding holidays, sales meeting, exhibitions, and all the other things that salespeople do within their role, you'll get a more accurate block of sales time. This often works out at around 200 days a year per person. By dividing the amount of time it's going to take to deliver the target by the available selling time per person, you can ascertain how many salespeople are required. This calculation also helps the Sales Manager illustrate to sales force members that their targets are achievable, as well as indicating the key ratios in that process. Knowing targets are achievable helps them to approach the task with positivity.

It's also important to optimise the effectiveness of the individuals within your sales force before you decide to recruit additional members. Typically you can achieve a **25% increase in output** just by focusing on optimising an existing sales force. It might sound like a no-brainer, but in our experience, companies rarely do it. I'll expand on this in the next chapter on 'Conduct'.

What often happens if companies look at how much each salesperson sells on average, and decide they need to grow their team by X amount in order to grow their business by Y amount. What if that business growth could be achieved by the existing team, without the expense of another employee? And, if it's decided that an extra salesperson is required, as well as the efficiency improvement measures, then you get the maximum impact from that additional person.

It's all about making the lowest common denominator as high as possible. Of course, when you do have new starts, another opportunity to maximise efficiency - and therefore revenue - is to ensure that the new person can get up to speed quickly, and start to deliver what's expected of them within the shortest possible period of time.

There are two key enablers for getting salespeople up to speed more quickly than they might do otherwise. The first is to give them an Activity Plan that says, "On average most of our people are able to do X. If they do 6 of these, 4 of those, 3 of those, 2 of those to get one of these." Explain to them that until they're able to create their own success plan, they need to work to the Activity Plan and all being well, they'll get where you need to be. It means they can hit the ground running knowing the quantity and direction of effort needed. Explain to them that it's this activity their basic salary covers.

Their basic salary is usually fixed and therefore the quantity of activity going in, the sales inputs as we call them, should also be fixed. The outputs of that activity are variable because we cannot 100% predict what will be sold. You can have a good idea but it's not exact science. Because the outputs are variable, you'd vary their overall commission level to reflect that. **Basic salaries are** not there to pay anyone's mortgage. They are there to ensure salespeople deliver an agreed constant level of key sales activities. And this is what the activity plan reflects.

The second enabler, an Ideal Opportunity Profile[2], then gives them a clear understanding of which deals you want them to be pursuing, which will also be the deals that maximise their available commission.

The SalesNet Model

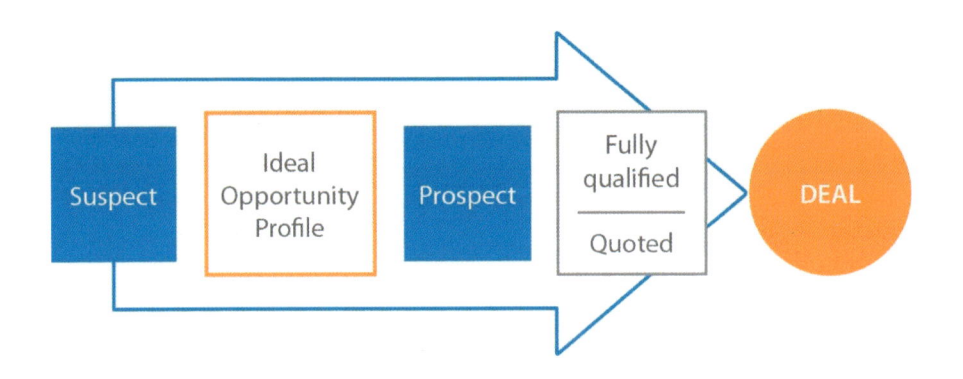

Suspect → Ideal Opportunity Profile → Prospect → Fully qualified / Quoted → DEAL

You should know all the numbers & ratios

In our experience, implementing these two key enablers from the outset shortens the amount of time it takes new starters to

---

[2] See appendix [Ideal Opportunity Profile]

get up to speed by up to half. Tell them exactly what you want and where to go to find it.

Case Study: Capacity

In the early days of our work with private equity backed business we were introduced to a food manufacturer whose sales had reached a plateau at around £13m pa. For every new customer they won, they lost revenue elsewhere, despite a sales force working flat out, often six days a week.

By analysing the sales process for new business as well as new from existing accounts (which was 80% of typical revenues), and then identifying each of the key activities needed to drive an opportunity from one end of the pipeline to the other (as well as the time each activity realistically took), we were able to help them drive an 18% increase in the top line in year one, followed by a further 15% in year two.

The key was identifying the tasks that the sales force had to complete to deliver a deal, and focussing them fully on these every week, whilst at the same time removing the other tasks that they completed but which were not core to the sales force or the sale – a typical example being sample preparation. The sales force chased these through the factory because if they didn't, they didn't get done in time.

By being able to show the consequences of this effort in lost sales time, the business was able to employ an additional person in a project management capacity, whose costs were less than a quarter of the additional margin on the revenue that could be won.

In other words, by establishing their current sales capacity they were able to see the most effective changes to increase it, so delivering the additional sales without initially recruiting any additional salespeople. They then had a solid platform to add new people to, which they subsequently did before selling the business very successfully, returning three times the money for the investors.

ⓘ TIPS TO AVOID THE TRAPS

- Is there a defined sales process? Is it documented? Is it in daily use by the majority of salespeople? Are the stages reflected in the pipeline?

- Are all of the key activities identified and the various dependencies mapped? Does everyone know their conversion ratios and average deal size?
- Does the sales management dashboard identify the 'upstream' indicators (new business visits, number and value of proposals issued etc.) of 'downstream' success (orders, contract wins)? If it does, are there target levels set for each of these? If there are, where did the targets come from?
- To what extent are 'blanket' KPIs in use across the team? How much variation from these 'standards' is there in practice?
- Does everyone know how much of which activities they have to deliver each week/month to hit their number?
- Is it obvious to management and the team members, which 'levers' could be pulled to enhance the current effectiveness of the sales operation, and what numerical improvement would this be expected to deliver?
- How long does it take for a new hire to start to deliver at 75% of target? Why?

Our Three 'C' methodology

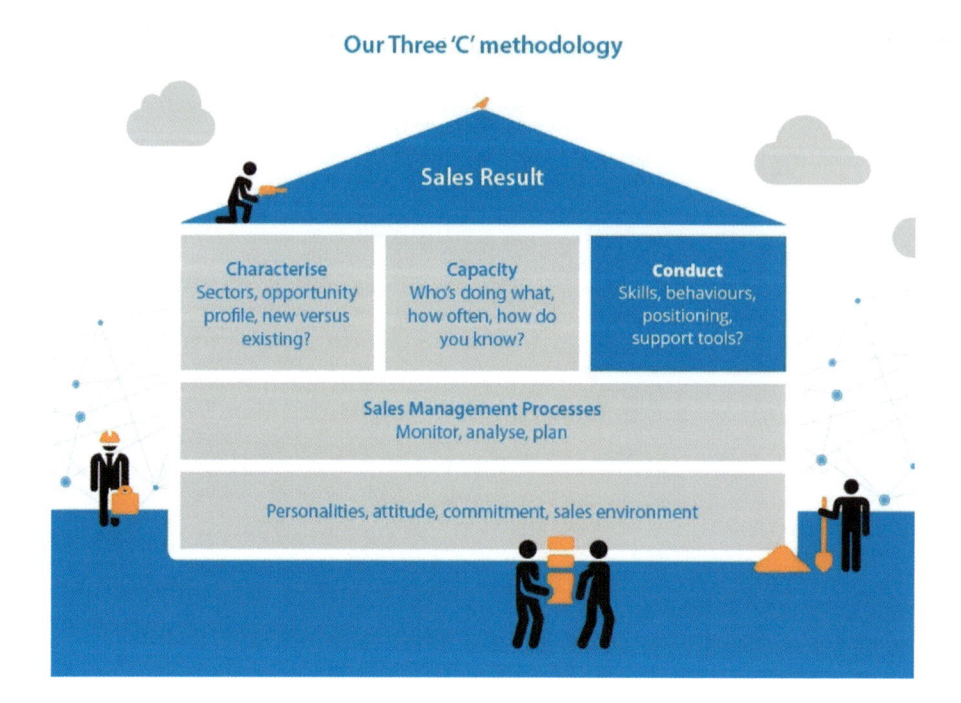

Characterise	Capacity	Conduct
Sectors, opportunity profile, new versus existing?	Who's doing what, how often, how do you know?	Skills, behaviours, positioning, support tools?

Sales Management Processes
Monitor, analyse, plan

Personalities, attitude, commitment, sales environment

1.3 Conduct

The third C stands for 'Conduct'; that is to say, the skills and behaviours that we expect the sales operation to display, to stand a fighting chance of winning the business that has been identified as desirable and achievable.

Characterise	Capacity	Conduct
Sectors, opportunity profile, new versus existing?	Who's doing what, how often, how do you know?	Skills, behaviours, positioning, support tools?

At the base of this is choosing the right people, which I'll elaborate on in Part 4: Human Capital, as the makeup of the sales force has a direct bearing on its ability to support the chosen strategy. Some businesses might decide they want their salespeople to act as both 'hunters' (chasing new opportunities) and 'farmers' (building relationships, typically within existing accounts) – though as I've mentioned already this doesn't really work, because people are usually much stronger at one or the other – whereas some businesses will opt for a proportion of farmers and a proportion of hunters within their sales force.

There are a number of other considerations, too. Do we need people that can sell over a two-year sale cycle, or do we need people that can sell over a two-week sale cycle? Is this a very consultative sale? Is it very soft? Many businesses never deliberately set these requirements. It's not necessarily that they don't know this stuff, though in some cases they don't. It's more that they have never had to think about it before, because no one has ever asked them the question.

If you evaluated the members of a sales force individually using a scale of one to 10, you'd likely find that most people are about a four in terms of effectiveness. This sounds quite low, but what it does mean is there's plenty of room for improvement. If, through improved training and management, the business can get them to a six or a seven, that's 50% improvement in conversion ratio, and you can imagine the sort of difference that would make.

Also, given that most sales forces operate at roughly the same level without such intervention, a business can suddenly raise their game 50% above the pack. This means that when there's a competitive situation, the sales force that is selling 50% better is likely to win more business, because they have taken the time and care to come up with a product or service solution that meets the client's needs, rather than just pitching something.

It's worth considering, however, that training alone is never enough. Even if a programme is really strong, it's often generic, and that doesn't work because you are asking salespeople to assimilate some new knowledge and immediately work out how to apply it in their world, with their customers, their tools, and their challenges, when they might not recognise the need to change in the first place.

It's help with the implementation that they need. If it were simply about finding out, then it would just be a case of reading a book about great selling, or researching online for a couple of days, but learning about selling well doesn't automatically translate into new and improved selling behaviours in the field.

It's the management, rather than the sales force, who should recognise the need to change, but it's not about telling salespeople what to do. That approach has very limited success. Where management can be effective is creating a practical implementation plan for applying new knowledge and any alteration in the way that the salesforce operates, enabling the sales people to more easily rise to the challenges of the new processes, knowing exactly how and why they should be doing things differently.

As well as being about the right people with the right goals, 'Conduct' is also about conveying the proposition effectively and persuasively. Why should customers buy from this company rather than any other? **Equipping a sales force with a clear company-sanctioned explanation about the product or service, its point of difference(s) against the competition, and above all else, what the customer might get from it that they could place real value on, will ensure that they can begin the core sales activity of asking the right questions.**

This is the heart of all consultative selling, and it's a skill few are naturals at. If a skill is defined as a learned behaviour that can be successfully repeated, then this one in particular requires constant practice and the most appropriate tools. Even great salespeople shouldn't be making up their own questions.

It's also important to consider an oft-forgotten aspect. The option of doing nothing. It's one thing to know the benefits of a product or service in relation to rival offerings, but how does it stack up against not making a buying decision at all? Obviously, the strength of the proposition is critical here. If a purchase can be delayed, then is it compelling enough? We would say that each company needs a suite of propositions which play to the various parts of the market that they want to sell into, and the key strengths of the business. You shouldn't let the sales force make that up, it should be devised by the marketing department.

You should view marketing as being upstream of sales, with sales executing one channel of the overall go-to-market strategy. Instead, often what we find is the sales force are doing the selling, while marketing just provides the brochures, runs the website, and comes up with the odd lead – many companies don't do marketing proper.

Of course, if you're going to do this marketing-sales relationship properly, there is a lot to do on the marketing side. It's not just a case of setting out the suite of propositions that the marketing team is responsible for either; it's the building of the brand. People often underestimate the value of a brand in the business-to-business world, but it's an important part of any sell.

This relationship between sales and marketing is a key reason why the lead criteria that were ascertained during the Characterise phase should be pinned down in a form that's easy to share, say, a written checklist. It's not just the sales force who need to understand what the right opportunity looks like, it's marketing, too.

Otherwise, if marketing is out there trying to find leads, and there isn't a really tight mechanism for measuring their quality, the Sales Director might ask the Marketing Director for more, only to get a confused response because there has never previously been solid communication about the exact characteristics of the type of leads that are required in order to close a significant proportion of them. We find this happens all the time.

However, if a Sales Director can say, "I want 50 leads a month and they have to tick all these boxes," marketing can work with that, whereas, "Get me some more, but not like those," will never result in an effective, efficient flow of good-quality leads.

On this point about marketing, we do understand that it is a much bigger subject than just being about lead generation - but that is outside the scope of this book.

Case Study: Conduct
We first worked with this industrial services provider pre-deal. We determined that their installation business was well run, and was able to identify all potential opportunities from strong market intelligence and then monitor them through the quotation and follow-up stages to an excellent win ratio. They weren't great at selling but the nature of the sales process meant it was much more of a numbers game – and they knew theirs!

The challenge, however, was how they were going to adapt to selling a new service, not just to their customer base but also to all of their competitors. They agreed with our assessment they needed a new sales process, new sales skills to support it, and a new suite of propositions designed specifically to sell the real value of their new offer. They asked us to help with the development of all of these since they represented a significant departure from their business-as-usual approach.

By understanding the significant differences between genuine value-based selling and the transactional approach they were used to, and then developing the in-house skills required to deliver it through a defined two stage sales process, we were able to help the company double monthly sales within six months to £42k pcm. Then, 18 months later, sales were running at over £80k pcm, more than compensating for a decline in the core installation market. Additionally, the demonstrable ability to adapt and broaden the range of services sold was instrumental in the business being sold two years later for 3.1x money and an IRR of 48%.

ⓘ TIPS TO AVOID THE TRAPS

- Is everyone crystal clear about what the various products/services actually deliver for each type of customer, in terms that they will definitely value? Is it written down anywhere?

- Is there a core questioning framework designed to elicit appropriate responses so that the prospect can see for themselves the true value delivered?
- Is everyone skilled at using it?
- Is there a succinct (and consistent) 'elevator pitch' in use by everyone?
- Is there a programme to enable a recently recruited salesperson (even a skilled one) to be confident of selling well for the new organisation right now?
- Is there programme for keeping sales skills fresh and up to date?
- What is in the sales toolkit and why?

# 2

The Keys To Maintenance & Continuous Improvement

Sales Management Skills & Processes

Overview

2.1 The Role Of The Sales Manager

2.2 Succession Planning

2.3 Key Account Planning

Our Three 'C' methodology

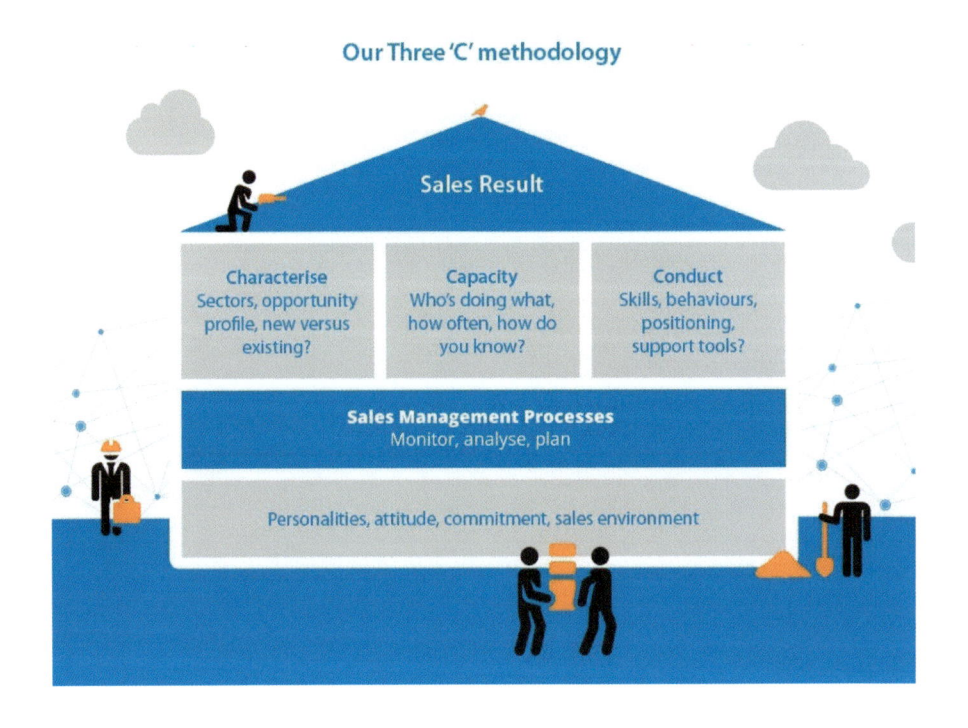

- **Sales Result**
- **Characterise**: Sectors, opportunity profile, new versus existing?
- **Capacity**: Who's doing what, how often, how do you know?
- **Conduct**: Skills, behaviours, positioning, support tools?
- **Sales Management Processes**: Monitor, analyse, plan
- Personalities, attitude, commitment, sales environment

2.1 The Role Of The Sales Manager

The key figures responsible for sales operations are the Sales Director and Sales Manager (or Managers). The differentiation between their roles can largely be summed up by the fact that one focuses on the strategic level, while the other is primarily tactical and operational[3].

---

[3] See appendix [Key Differences Between Sales Directors & Sales Managers]

After the 'Characterise' phase, during which we pin down exactly the sort of business that will deliver the target revenue, the Sales Director devises a plan to meet expectations regarding the split of new and existing clients, and the responsibility for executing sales activity filters down to the Sales Manager. It might sound obvious, but sales management is, by definition, about managing people. So rather than simply being an excellent salesperson who's risen to the top, those in managerial positions need the requisite set of leadership, coaching and communication skills to be genuinely successful.

A Sales Management Framework

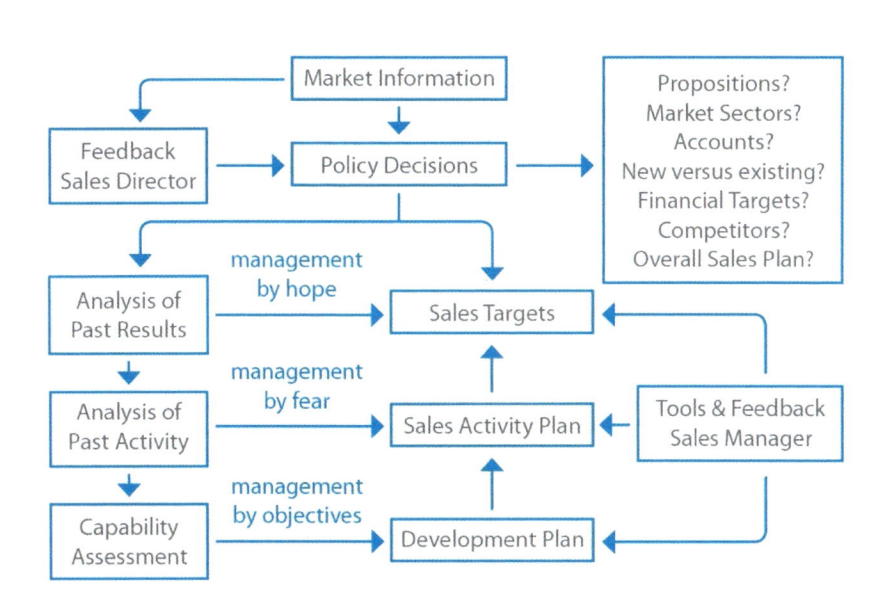

```
                          ┌─────────────────────┐        ┌──────────────────────┐
                          │ Market Information  │        │    Propositions?     │
                          └─────────┬───────────┘        │    Market Sectors?   │
┌──────────────┐                    ▼                    │      Accounts?       │
│  Feedback    │          ┌─────────────────────┐        │ New versus existing? │
│Sales Director│─────────▶│  Policy Decisions   │───────▶│  Financial Targets?  │
└──────┬───────┘          └─────────┬───────────┘        │     Competitors?     │
       │                            │                    │  Overall Sales Plan? │
       ▼              management    ▼                    └──────────────────────┘
┌──────────────┐      by hope   ┌─────────────┐
│ Analysis of  │───────────────▶│Sales Targets│◀────────────────┐
│ Past Results │                └─────────────┘                 │
└──────┬───────┘                       ▲                        │
       ▼              management       │                 ┌──────────────────┐
┌──────────────┐      by fear   ┌─────────────────┐      │ Tools & Feedback │
│ Analysis of  │───────────────▶│Sales Activity Plan│◀──│  Sales Manager   │
│ Past Activity│                └─────────────────┘      └──────────────────┘
└──────┬───────┘                       ▲                        │
       ▼              management       │                        │
┌──────────────┐      by objectives ┌──────────────────┐        │
│  Capability  │───────────────────▶│ Development Plan │◀───────┘
│  Assessment  │                    └──────────────────┘
└──────────────┘
```

43

Often, there's an inherent weakness in promoting a top-performing salesperson to managerial level. Firstly, you lose all the sales that person used to bring you, and secondly, you're relying on that person with very little, if any, training in sales management to work out how to codify what they did that was good and then get everybody else to copy it, if they can. This skill isn't something that people are born with.

It's quite possible a salesperson might never be a very good Sales Manager because they simply don't know what 'good' looks like. They don't know what the art of the possible is, and there isn't a course for them to go on that they can learn all of that from. We see lots of people who aren't wilfully doing the wrong thing, they just don't know what they don't know. As well as the right skills and knowledge, Sales Managers also need to have the time to properly manage the proportion of the field sales force that reports directly to them, so it's important that this does not total more than eight to 10 staff.

Field accompaniment
If there are too many salespeople under the direction of one Sales Manager, he or she will likely end up desk-bound, and that's not what the job is about. Of course, it depends on the specifics of the business (if you're running a call centre, for

example, then desk time is likely to be higher), but a good Sales Manager should be spending at least 50% of their time with 'their' salespeople. They should help them understand what they're doing in relation to the sales strategy, guide them, coach them, improve them, and help them understand how to get the most out of the tools at their disposal.

Even with the best talent, you can't simply train them up and let them do their thing. They need a manager's perspective to keep them on track, and enhance their performance in a way that's relevant to the wider business objectives. Consider other highly trained professionals, for example, footballers, soldiers, police, airline pilots. They undergo continual training and guidance throughout their careers, to ensure optimum results. Effective sales forces are no different. They need continual leadership and development to ensure the highest standards can be maintained.

It's about that sales process again. If the sales operation is a factory whose output is orders, doesn't it make sense to take a regular look around and makes sure its all working properly?

A good rule of thumb is for a Sales Manager to spend a day a week in the field with each of their people every month. This is why the maximum number for one manager's allocation of people should be 10, since this represents two weeks' worth of work on its own, before you factor in meetings, recruitment and all the other tasks which make up the role's responsibilities. Without this sort of close contact, there's no chance that a Sales Manager can effectively manage today's resource to deliver today's number, let alone develop that resource to deliver tomorrow's number.

We often hear Sales Managers say that they employ grown-ups who should know how to do the job and don't need to be 'micro-managed', but our experience is that everybody benefits from effective sales management, no matter how experienced they think themselves. Anyone who thinks the time for learning and development is over should retire immediately!

On this point, Sales Managers should obviously carry out regular performance reviews with each member of their team. Once they have the individual data to illustrate each salesperson's performance at each stage of the sales process, sales management has the basis for an opportunity for both sides to review progress and assess the room for improvement. This might involve specific skills training, or perhaps learning from others who are better at certain stages of the sales process, or it could involve changes to the way the sales process is implemented for a particular individual[4]. It shouldn't be only about the revenue numbers and should never be only about those who are perceived to be failing.

This might sound like a straightforward and sensible approach to maximising sales performance, but it's surprising how many sales organisations – even those with multi-million pound turnovers – aren't set up this way. More often than not, training is seen as a once-a-year occurrence, and for the other 51 weeks salespeople are pretty much left to their own devices, and the only benchmark of their performance is their output.

If the output doesn't marry up with the expectation, it's often a few months before it becomes clear there's a problem. By then it's all too late. With a more supportive, attentive approach to people management, issues can be identified and fixed before they can have a significant detrimental impact on the sales force's ability to achieve its targets.

---

[4] See appendix [In-Call Assessment Forms]

Managers, trainers and coaches

Something else that is widely misunderstood is the use and value of coaching. In my opinion, most of Britain doesn't understand what coaching is, and how coaches differ from trainers and managers. Coaching is about helping people realise their full potential. And while it's not widely practised in business-to-business sales operations, it should be. It should be an essential part of any Sales Manager's skill set.

Core coaching skills

- Trust
- Using intuition
- Asking great questions
- Giving great feedback
- Active listening

Reference: The Coaching Manual by Julie Starr, Pearson Books 2nd Edition 2008, p.103

The senior management team should be setting out the expectation that coaching will be an integral part of the Sales Manager's role, and providing the sales department with the resources it needs to implement this aspect of people management. This will optimise staff performance, which in turn optimises revenue. It may sound like a no-brainer when reduced down to the basics in this way, but while it may be common sense, it's not currently common practice.

Managing the sales pipeline

The clearly defined sales process that we discussed in the 'Capacity' part of the 3 Cs chapter can be represented in visual form, often in Excel, although most CRM tools include the means to do this. Visual data helps to track the progress of the various sales opportunities informs management decision-making. It's the Sales Manager's job to manage this pipeline.

Each sales step in the pipeline often has a different weighted value, often subjectively awarded by the sales force, and herein lies the problem. A subjective decision about weighting simply doesn't result in data that will stand up to scrutiny, so it's important to set a more formal, objective set of criteria.

Sometimes, and this is most common pre-deal, the weighting will be a somewhat arbitrary percentage chance of winning, often devised by accountants, which isn't illuminating unless the business in question has hundreds or even thousands of orders going through every month, and is fairly predictable in terms of the type of sales being made. The worth of a sales pipeline can't accurately be evaluated in this way, especially if there are more complex criteria that might have an impact (for example, if big projects are less likely to be won).

This approach is passable when it comes to financial modelling, but simply won't cut it in the real world of sales management. You can't simply say, "We win 40% of what we quote for, so a million worth of potential sales will convert into £400,000." It's nonsense because sales is a binary game. You can't win 40% of one job, and you could win all of the work in the pipeline or you could lose it all.

Also, while many businesses will fill their sales pipeline with every enquiry, it's more revealing to only include genuine opportunities. This will help you assess each possible piece of business for viability when tested against the objective criteria that were set out in the 'Characterise' phase[5].

In reality, what most businesses do is put every little enquiry into the system, and no-one ever goes back and qualifies them again or cleans the pipeline, so five years later it has apparently got 10

---

[5] See appendix [Ideal Opportunity Profile]

million pounds' worth of opportunity in it. In actual fact you might only be able to close about a much smaller proportion, if only you knew. One of the disciplines a Sales Manager needs to implement, apart from robust forecasting methodology, is that everything's qualified before it goes in, and everything's qualified at each stage in the sales cycle, so the pipeline will reflect the accurate sales situation (and enable the Sales Manager to know whether the growth ambitions are feasible).

A Sales Manager should also know what the conversion rate is from each stage to the next stage, not just from quote to order or from initial inquiry to order, which is more commonly what is measured. It's useful, of course, but there's a lot that happens in the middle and to get a clearer picture you need to tease out some more data. You might have some serious problems in the middle that that would be masked if you didn't measure at each stage. With more detail, you can tackle any problems with greater precision, which of course leads to speedier resolution and improved performance.

The Sales Management Dashboard

One of the most useful tools a Sales Manager can adopt is a dashboard which collates all the indicators of whether the sales strategy is running to plan. Most have a very crude version, which simply equates to the size of the pipeline and the order cover, and they're not really Key Performance Indicators in themselves.

If you've worked out your sales capacity properly, your dashboard can then help you say, "Right, we would normally expect to deliver X in this month. This means we should complete 10 first-stage meetings across the team, five second-stage meetings and three negotiation-stage meetings", for example. If you know what you should have been doing, then you can measure what you actually did and comparing the two gives you a genuine KPI. You are then in a position to effect any remedial action *before there is a significant impact on the order book.*

A professional dashboard can also help the Sales Manager to identify areas of the sales process that could be improved, in order to make the operation more efficient and effective[6]. Once the ratios at each stage of the pipeline have been identified, it's possible to review them and consider how to realise improvements in output. For example, it might be that the

---

[6] The illustration shows a simple dashboard, demonstrating some of the genuine KPIs of sales operations. A relevant illustration of this nature should also be in the board pack for every growth-focused private equity-backed business.

quality of the proposals needs an upgrade, or the quality of the initial targeting, or the quality of the leads. By seeing all of the appropriate levers that might be pulled, it's much easier to decide which one is going to deliver the best result.

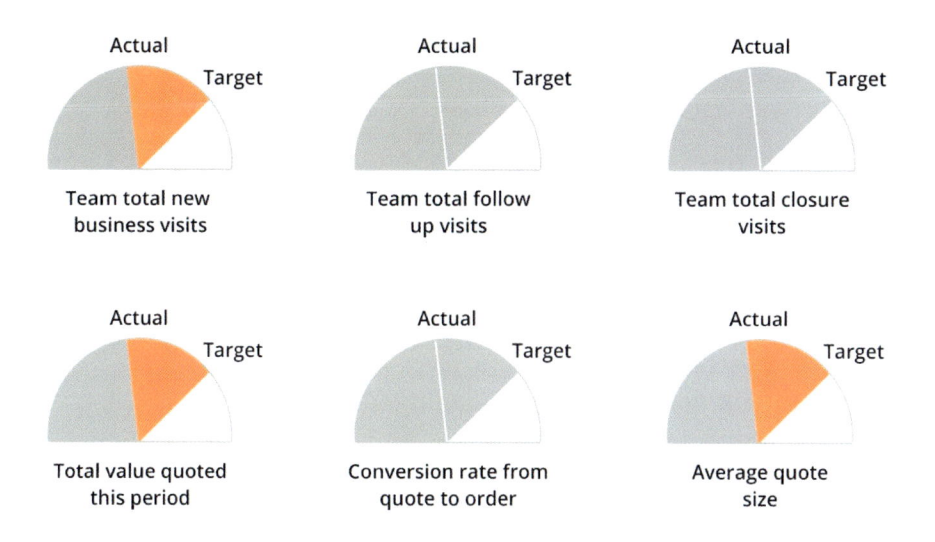

Actual / Target	Actual / Target	Actual / Target
Team total new business visits	Team total follow up visits	Team total closure visits
Total value quoted this period	Conversion rate from quote to order	Average quote size

As you can see in this example monthly dashboard, the first line marks the actual number hit, and the second line marks the target number. If all targets are hit, there will be no deficit - both the actual and target segments will be green. In this case, you have nothing to worry about. However if targets are not met, the difference will be highlighted in red. Then you know you need to take action, and can analyse why these leading indicator targets were missed before deciding on the best cause of action.

The real learning here is that you've got a target. So many businesses miss this yet it's the most important part of any dashboard; it's the definition of measuring performance. Since the private equity investments in the mid-market are always predicated on top line growth as the main driver of shareholder value, you need to know what the KPIs need to look like in future years (as opposed to comparing them to some point in the past) to deliver the planned growth. Doing better than this time last year might indicate growth, but is it enough?

Of course, although it often can, this isn't always a process that will yield immediate results. Changing the way people sell to improve the conversion ratio isn't something that can be done in two days. Developing a new proposal might take a month. If a sales cycle is six months long anyway, it's clearly going to take some time before the impact of today's improvements will show in the figures. But developing today's resource for tomorrow requires a sustainable solution, not a quick fix, so a long-term view should certainly be taken.

2.2 Succession Planning

It's inevitable that in any sales department that there will be a turnover of staff. Obviously, a very high turnover is undesirable and often indicates problems either with the recruitment or the existing culture, but even in a high-performing culture where everything's going well, people will come and go. There will always be those moving on for personal reasons, because they simply fancy a change, or because they think the grass is greener.

But a very low turnover of staff can also indicate a less-than-optimal sales operation. A good manager should always be looking to improve the performance of the group as a whole, and therefore if the bar is always being raised, there will always come a point when somebody can't or won't deliver the required level of performance. It may be right, therefore, that they see the writing on the wall and they move on to somewhere else, which is a positive action for all involved. However, if they don't make that decision for themselves, the Sales Manager may have to make it for them.

Under-performing salespeople should always (with due process, of course) be rooted out if they prove to be incapable of achieving the necessary standards, or are unwilling to make the necessary changes in order to do so. This is essential to maintain high morale within the sales force. The first people to notice when a sales executive isn't pulling their weight are that person's colleagues. It's not their manager, even with the very best practice and all the right tools in place.

Now one of the challenges for the manager is what do they then do about it? Often for reasons that make good sense at the time, they prevaricate over the best course of action. There are various options to try and get them back on track, such as an initial conversation to get to the bottom of the issue, coaching, support, but at some point, a line has to be drawn. If you can't change the people, you need to change the people.

Most Sales Managers and Sales Directors actually take too long to make this sort of decision, and they often underestimate the negative impact this delay can have on the rest of the department, and also on the sales force's respect for their seniors. Since confidence is a key part of selling, a manager who is slow to respond can even risk their whole sales force underperforming as a result of their inability to do something about one individual.

Recruiting new talent

One of the secrets to more easily finding new salespeople to fill vacancies is to cultivate a sort of 'subs bench' before the need for a new employee actually arises. The most successful Sales Managers are always interviewing. Not just to identify potential new starts, but also to gain information about competitors, which is surprisingly easy to do when a candidate thinks they might get offered a job!

It's good practice to always have people earmarked to bring into the organisation when required, sometimes at short notice. This speedy turnaround matters a lot in sales. The under performance of an outgoing employee is likely to have negatively impacted on targets for a while, and there will be time required for a new start to get up to speed and start working at optimum effectiveness, so this sub-par period should be kept as short as possible.

2.3 Key Account Planning

If a significant proportion of planned revenue comes from what might be termed 'key' accounts, there are some specific sales management processes that you will need in order to ensure success.

The first step is to define what a key account is, in line with the overall sales policy, and the target business policy that you've already characterized. It's not simply that key accounts give you a significant share of revenue you wouldn't want to lose. That's a factor, of course, but often it's more to do with the scope for cross- or up-selling, because they're a strategically important business in their industry, or because they have significant growth potential. Whatever the size of a business, customers who are well-placed to grow significantly represent a much better key account than customers who will place a huge one-off order.

You also have to bear in mind the extent to which a company can be a profitable account, not just on the margins that you sell and subsequently close out, but the cost to serve that account.

Some accounts might be a big part of your revenue, but if you actually sat down and worked out what the total cost of serving that account is - especially in sales time - it might not justify the small margins that you get on a big volume. People rarely do these calculations, but they're important.

The second step is to decide who's going to run these key accounts. Because looking after such customers requires a mix of hunting and farming, you might need a team of people to ensure the right mix of skills. Account management is largely about farming, but you do need somebody looking for the opportunities, as well as servicing the incoming requirements. If you simply respond to what customers want then you're never going to get the growth that you've identified as possible. You might find both types of activity can be fulfilled by the same person, but it is a real challenge to find such an all-rounder - the bottom line is, one way or the other, you need the appropriate resource to hunt when required and farm when required (as well carry out the admin, and perform other daily account management tasks).

The third step is to decide upon the best processes to make sure the projected growth can be delivered, and the appropriate KPIs can be captured. You'll need some kind of account planning process document, which is in-depth and strategic in its outlook (rather than tactical), although there will of course be a series of actions detailed within it.

Even in well-deployed key account management methodologies, of which there are several, the real risk is that people become too focused on what the business is trying to achieve, and they don't spend enough time demonstrating to the key account customer that they're really trying to understand what the customer's objectives are. Often you'll find a key account plan simply lists key customers, lists what the company sells to them, lists what the company wants to sell to them, and lists the actions that are going to be taken to make that happen.

Job done? Well, not exactly. The bit that's missing in all that is what the customer is trying to achieve. Where are they trying to get to? Forget what you're selling them; let's understand their plans and objectives. You'll then have a very different conversation with them, because they see you as part of their future, not just somebody trying to sell them something.

🛈 *TIPS TO AVOID THE TRAPS*

- Does sales management spend a day per month in the field with each member of the sales force, *even the strong performers?*
- How many quota-carrying direct reports does the sales manager have?
- Is forecasting down to 'gut feel' and subjectivity? Is there a process, and how accurate is it? Is the size and shape of future revenues clearly outlined in the board pack?
- Does management know big the pipeline has to be to succeed and why that is the case?
- What is the current rate of sales staff turnover?
- Was a salesperson fired in the last 12 months? Why?
- How are new sales staff sourced and inducted?
- How long would it take to replace the top performer?
- How are key accounts identified? Is there process to protect and develop them?
- What does the key account plan look like? How often is it used?

3

The Secrets To Outperforming The Plan

Importance Of A High-Performing Culture

Overview

3.1 Creating a High-Performing Culture

3.2 Setting Targets for a High-Performing Culture

3.3 High-Performance Meetings & Field Visits

Our Three 'C' methodology

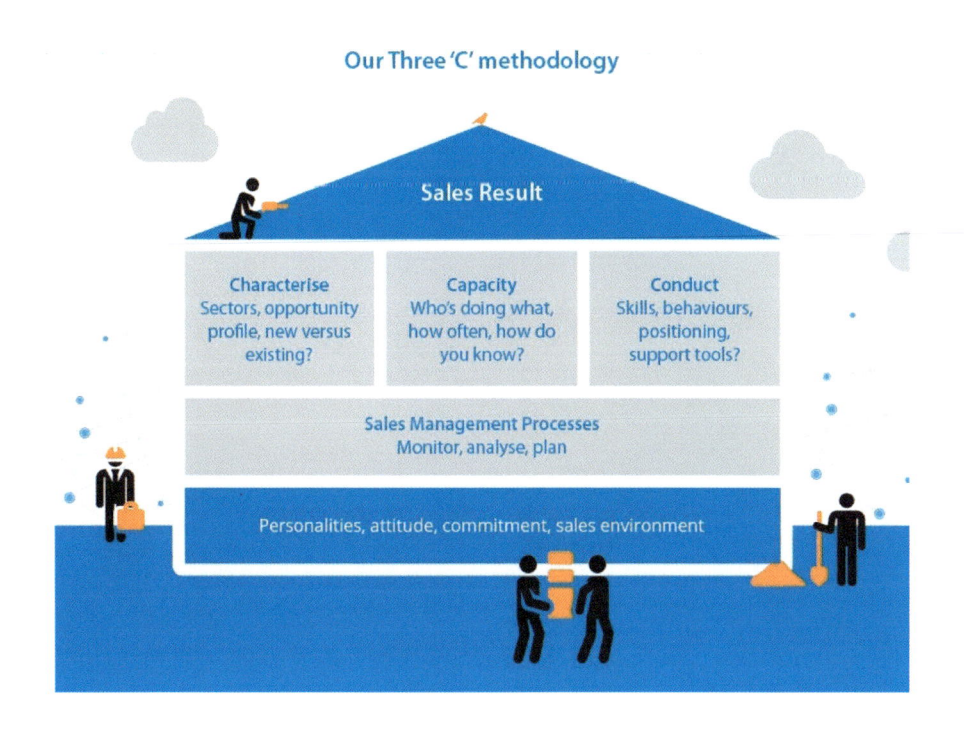

- **Sales Result**
- **Characterise**: Sectors, opportunity profile, new versus existing?
- **Capacity**: Who's doing what, how often, how do you know?
- **Conduct**: Skills, behaviours, positioning, support tools?
- **Sales Management Processes**: Monitor, analyse, plan
- Personalities, attitude, commitment, sales environment

3.1 Creating a High-Performing Culture

We're pretty unequivocal about our responses to most questions from private equity investors, but there are two to which the answer is most likely to be, "It depends." The first one is, "What's the most appropriate sales structure?" Other than keeping the scope of a Sales Manager's responsibility to a maximum of eight to 10 people, there isn't actually much to say in terms of universal good practice. It really all depends on the people within the sales department at the time, and what the business is trying to achieve.

The second of these questions is "What's the best commission scheme?" Again, the answer is, "It depends," but there is some good practice to be followed.

Commission schemes and remuneration packages

Most successful commission schemes have a base salary no greater than two-thirds of the On Target Earnings (OTE) and ideally is closer to half. Another important element is an accelerator for over a 100% performance, so that people are less likely to sandbag orders in a quarter or a year in order to achieve a particular bonus. If there's an accelerator, it doesn't stop this practice, but it does provide a disincentive. It's also good practice to ensure people are not paid commission on everything they sell, but have a hurdle they have to clear before they start to earn commission. Typically, this is 75-80% of the target, so that the salespeople have, at the bare minimum, covered the costs of their employment before you start to pay them commission. Finally, always make sure that any commission scheme is based around gross margin, and not revenue, if you can.

Margin £ **Reward**

The commission scheme should never be used to drive behaviour, but instead to reward the behaviour you want to encourage. It's a subtle difference but it matters. To do this, you link your commission payments to all the things that matter. For example, you might decide to not pay out commission unless all of an employee's CRM records are up to date, or first make sure that the agreed level of activity required to deliver the projected results has happened.

These checks and balances help avoid the problem of salespeople gaming the system in order to generate maximum commission, rather than putting effort into a more sustainable strategy to deliver the required business growth. It doesn't mean the people aren't still focused on the money, but it does mean they will get all the other things done.

While salespeople may be focused on the money to some extent, it's actually a popular misconception that they are *all* motivated by money. In our experience only about 10% of the people that we come across are genuinely only interested in the cash. Some of them want to be seen as number one, some of them want to be seen as a top performer, some of them want to be seen as a really good, reliable person, while some of them want to be seen as the next Sales Manager and so on. Just as with any other department, you'll find the whole range of reasons for human motivation within the same department.

League tables

This is one of the reasons that league tables don't work. I often use the Premier League as an analogy. Even if you don't know much about football, you could probably arrange the names of the 20 teams into the top, middle, and bottom third, without knowing much else. You'd simply ask yourself "Which is the biggest club? Who's got the most money?" and that will dictate where they finish, largely (most years!).

Sales league tables are the same. People like to think that if they publish a league table, the ones near the bottom will decide to raise their game and somehow miraculously outperform what they used to do, but that's based on the assumption that they want to be at the top, when actually they might not. In many cases, what they actually want to do is avoid getting relegated!

Some salespeople simply don't want to be in the bottom 10%, and the existence of a league table won't get them to be number one, because they would have to want that in the first place. They might actually just want to carry on and do a reasonable job, more or less on target, and do okay. A league table is a very blunt instrument. We see, for example, salespeople on a £35k basic, and if they do really well they can earn £40k and they are happy, hard-working and motivated. If they were purely money-orientated, they'd definitely be working somewhere else.

Sales staff motivation

Money-only motivated staff often aren't the best choice, either. A sales force of hungry alpha males who are inclined towards aggressive competition and want to be number one may seem like they might deliver high performance, but in actual fact they are often easily bored, don't stay long, are not very loyal, and rarely share the values of the organisation.

That said, it's important not to swing the balance too far the other way. Sales is not a team game, so shared targets rarely work. Everybody should have an individual target for which they are accountable. Group targets, whilst they might foster a collaborative work ethic on one level, almost always lead to overall lower levels of performance than would have been the case otherwise.

Good salespeople manage to get the whole business to work with them despite individual targets. They're not mavericks, they're not loners, but ultimately their number one loyalty is to have done their number, and everything else comes second. With a team mentality, you tend to get everybody performing at an average between the highest and the lowest, and this makes it difficult to weed out the people who aren't really contributing.

In reality, there's a whole range of things that you need to be aware of if you're going to get salespeople consistently performing, and if you're going to create that high-performing culture. The key is to recognise that salespeople are exactly that - people. Finding what 'presses their buttons' at an individual level is the trick and the ultimate art of management of course. Personality profiling is a good way to understand the various different characters and motivations within a sales force, and it also helps to reveal how a manager should modify their style to extract the best performance from each employee.

It can also be worth measuring employee engagement, to investigate the cultural status quo before beginning to make changes. We tend to use the Gallup Q12, which is a series of questions designed to test whether employees feel valued, supported, and encouraged. Research has shown that organisations where they have high levels of employee engagement, on average, deliver 17% better returns than organizations that don't, which is a significant figure by anybody's standards, especially when you consider it can be achieved just by making small changes.

3.2 Managing Change for a High-Performing Culture

So, what does a high-performing culture look like? It often depends on a number of factors including the specific aims of the business (in other words, high-performing compared to what?) and, in particular, the commitment from senior management to making it happen. The key is consistency of values and beliefs across the workforce, as a solid basis upon which to set operational excellence. This is far from easy to create of course, but is always worth the effort.

Values and beliefs

The Seven Levels is formed on the idea that there are natural hierarchies in the processes of change, with each level being a prerequisite for the next one's success. Underpinning everything, 'purpose' involves understanding why change is required, layered over with 'identity', which is about whether change reflects the self.

The 7 psychological levels

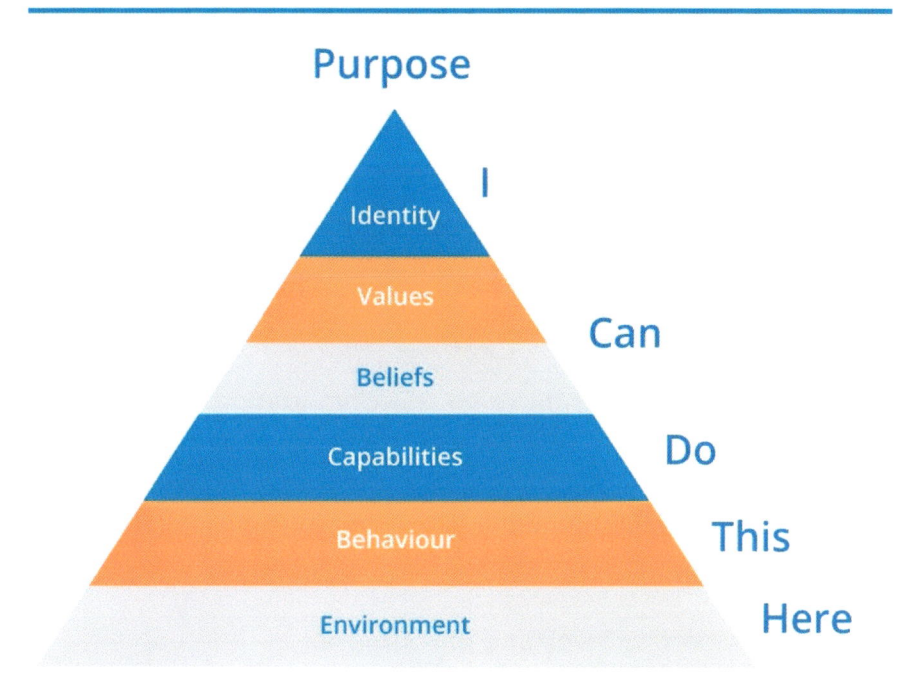

```
            Purpose
              /\
             /  \
            /Identity\      I
           /----------\
          /   Values   \
         /--------------\   Can
        /    Beliefs     \
       /------------------\
      /    Capabilities    \  Do
     /----------------------\
    /      Behaviour         \ This
   /--------------------------\
  /        Environment         \ Here
 /_____\
```

So, for example, if you tried to create a high-performing culture by simply redesigning the office in a funky way, you might find it boosts morale and initially has a positive impact. But while everyone comes in on a Monday, everything looks different and they're excited, by Tuesday they get used to it, and only a week later it's become the norm. Tackling 'environment' alone might change the way people feel, but it rarely changes the way people do things, because the other levels need to be in place first.

If you can start to think about getting the right values and beliefs in place, then you can make sure people have got the right capability, then you'll start to get the behaviours you need... in which case the environment simply needs to reinforce those. On its own, it doesn't change anything.

Similarly, if you try to persuade a sales force of farmers that they should now be hunting, it rarely works because their perception of themselves as a contributor to the organization is not as a hunter. There's no point in putting them in that position, even with the right training and commission scheme, because further up the pyramid there's a weakness - you have to address the change at the 'identity' level (and of course below that too).

Another simple example is if you've got a sales force that collectively keeps moaning about their company cars, you could agree to get them a better one. For a week they'll all be delighted, and stop moaning, but soon it would normalize, and they'd start complaining again. This sort of behaviour usually hints at a much deeper problem, which can't be fixed simply by changing the car.

Dig deeper, and it'll likely boil down to how they see their role, how important they think they are to the organisation (hence why they want a better car), how important they think they are to their clients, and how important they think sales is generally. If you don't address the deeper issues you won't create a high-performing culture. Instead you'll have the same people moaning in a better car!

Of course, it goes without saying that any recruitment activity required should be designed to employ people whose values and beliefs already naturally align with those of the organisation as a whole. However, very rarely - especially in private equity backed businesses which are not startups - do you recruit everybody that you want to work with. You might recruit some new people, but fundamentally you're inheriting a team that you have to make better. This is where you need some kind of mechanism to make sure they are on board properly, at the deepest level, before you start getting them to do things differently.

3.3 Setting Targets For A High-Performing Culture

It's not really possible to discuss what constitutes a high-performing culture without mentioning targets. In sales you're always going to have a target and it should always be an individual one as we've already said. Setting the right target is imperative. There's sometimes a temptation to set the same target for each area, in an attempt at fairness, but in reality this approach is far from fair.

For example, if one person is selling in the North East, and another's territory is in the South East, the idea that there will be the same amount of business is bizarre, given the major differences in the local economies - if the targets are the same, the salesperson based in the prosperous South East will smash it, while their more northerly-based counterpart will never get close to it.

We've had several clients who have managed to create an inequality of this sort precisely by attempting to ensure equality. I encourage them to consider how the person in the more challenging territory feels about never having hit target. No matter what your area of business or your role, you want to feel you're being successful, and in sales one of the measures of success is whether or not you've delivered your number.

A client told me that a certain salesperson has consistently failed to deliver their number, but that they wouldn't consider firing them, because they know that the target can't be achieved in that region. My response is always to suggest they make the target more realistic, and specific to each territory, because when people succeed in reaching their target, everything they sell after that is easy. Mentally, the salesperson is in a different place. In fact, unrealistic targets usually cause people to switch off very quickly. Some might remain positive, and see how close they can get, but quite a lot will simply see the impossibility, and so decide not to bother. Their rationale is that whether they make the effort or not, they will still fail.

- Realistic
- Achievable
- Positive
- Individual

Equal opportunity targets

It's best to create a target which can be achieved by somebody operating at a reasonably effective level. One tactic we've seen work very well is to make sure that anybody who's any good achieves their annual number by the end of Q3. That particular client paid their sales force extra commission once they were over 100%. It was all fully costed, so they weren't giving away more money than necessary, and it meant that for the final quarter almost their whole team was in a place where they were successful and, crucially felt it. This had a significant impact on their mindset and the overall approach to winning business.

As a result, they sold more than they would have done if they could all just about reach their target by the end of the year. It's interesting to see how confidence can make a huge difference when someone is sitting in front of a prospect. If they're having a difficult time, and every client they're trying to land isn't playing ball, then there's the possibility of a sense of desperation, and people pick up on this. Nobody wants to buy from someone who's desperate; everybody wants to buy from someone who's successful. Isn't it always the way that when there's little business, you can't seem to convert those leads, and then when your sales ledger is looking full you get even more orders coming in?

Clearly, you must be careful where you set the bar. But if you understand what your sales capacity is, and you have a good idea of the salesperson output expectation, you can calculate a realistic 'stretch' to ensure achievability without making it too easy.

3.4 High-Performance Meetings & Field Visits

Clients often ask me how often sales meetings should be held, but there's actually no right answer to that other than 'regularly'. It's also important to have a clear idea of their purpose from the start. Most sales staff have sat in the sort of meeting in which each person takes a turn at explaining how things are going for them, and - let's be honest - often there's a fairly low level of engagement, with people only paying proper attention when it's their turn to speak.

It's far better to do this type of reporting on an individual basis, with just the salesperson and their manager, rather than involving the whole sales force. It's better to only get everyone in the same room for things like motivational sessions, delivering new product or sales information, training, and general positive feedback - I'd certainly avoid giving any negative news in a sales meeting, too (if bad news cannot be avoided, it's more appropriate to discuss it via one-on-one communication, not in a meeting with the whole sales force present). Keep sales meetings short, to the point, and always about confidence, and motivation.

Similarly, I'm usually asked how frequently a Sales Manager should go out in the field with their sales force. You might hear a manager say that they don't need to go out with their salespeople because they trust them to do a good job, but it's not actually about trust, or even whether they're doing a good job - in fact it's just as important to visit with your best performers as it is to go along with those who need more help and support.

Everyone should receive the same opportunity for their manager's attention, even if the time spent together is for different reasons. It might even be to find out why a particular salesperson is managing to close more deals than the others, in which case it's valuable intelligence that bears sharing with the other members of the sales force. Also, if you only visit with those who are struggling, you create a great deal of negativity around the prospect of a manager's field visit, where in actual fact it should be viewed as a constructive, positive experience.

Again, it's all a part of creating a high-performing culture, and Sales Managers shouldn't be tied to a desk. They have to go out with each part of their operation all of the time. We've already suggested a good rule of thumb is for them to be with each member of their team one day a month.

4

If You Can't Change The People, Change The People

Human Capital

Overview

4.1 Getting The Right Talent

4.2 An Induction Process For Faster Performance

4.3 Summary

Our Three 'C' methodology

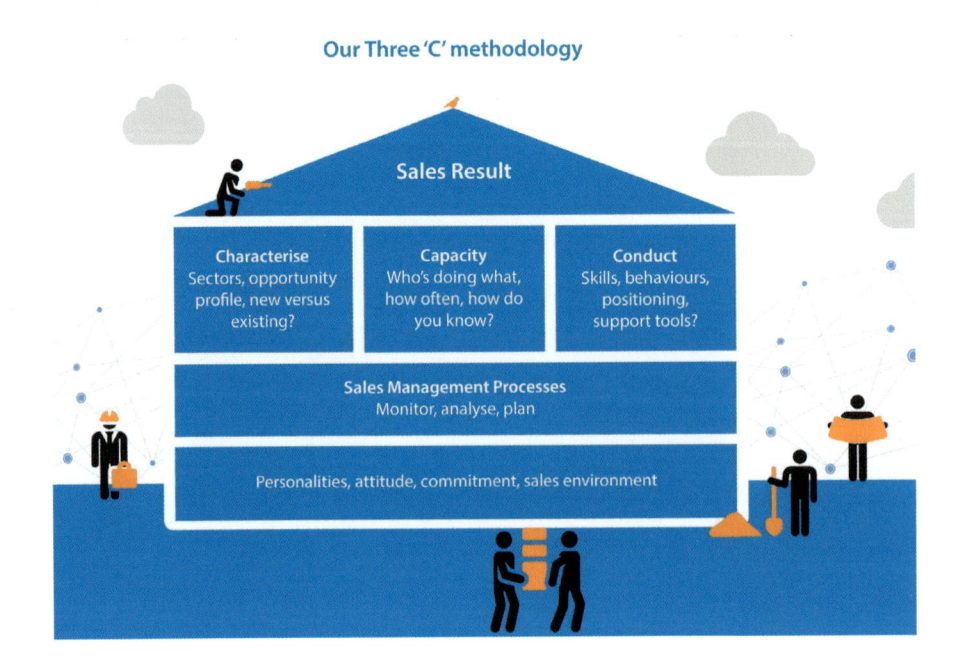

Sales Result

Characterise	Capacity	Conduct
Sectors, opportunity profile, new versus existing?	Who's doing what, how often, how do you know?	Skills, behaviours, positioning, support tools?

Sales Management Processes
Monitor, analyse, plan

Personalities, attitude, commitment, sales environment

4.1 Getting The Right Talent

Of course, it's beyond the scope of this book to detail best practice in all human resource processes, but in order to keep a sales operation performing well there are a number of aspects regarding recruitment and training that should be given particular attention – without the right people, even the best-planned sales growth simply won't materialise. Ultimately, if you've got weak people in a great process, the results will be okay and if you've got great people in a weak process, results will be okay. But with great people and a great process, that's when sales performance can soar.

The business as a whole should have a robust mechanism for finding members of the sales force at all levels. You could argue, quite rightly, that this should be true of every employee a company ever hires, but given the pivotal role of sales in revenue generation and growth and the specific skills sets required to optimise sales operations effectiveness, it's critical within this department in order to maximise the potential for revenue. It's also worth remembering it's not just the Sales Manager's job to hire well, it's the board's job to hire the right Sales Director in the first place.

Testing for aptitude and attitude

While we don't do recruitment – after all, there are a lot of well-connected headhunting and recruitment companies able to find applicants efficiently and speedily - we do support the process. We use our specific knowledge about high-performing sales operations to identify which candidates are likely to bring with them the right skills and aptitudes to achieve the high standards we'd expect from the optimised sales function. Our assessment centres test the qualities and approaches that the best people need to become an outstanding Sales Director, Manager or Executive, for example, leadership and teamwork.

One of the reasons that we recommend testing innate preferences and abilities is because it's difficult to pin down an accurate picture of performance in previous roles. As we've covered already, the number of companies approaching sales in the optimum manner is in the minority, and there are no recognised formal qualifications in sales. Largely seen as an art rather than a science, a lot of sales recruitment is based on a belief that personality has a great bearing on ability, and while that is true, it's actually only part of the story.

You are what you think about

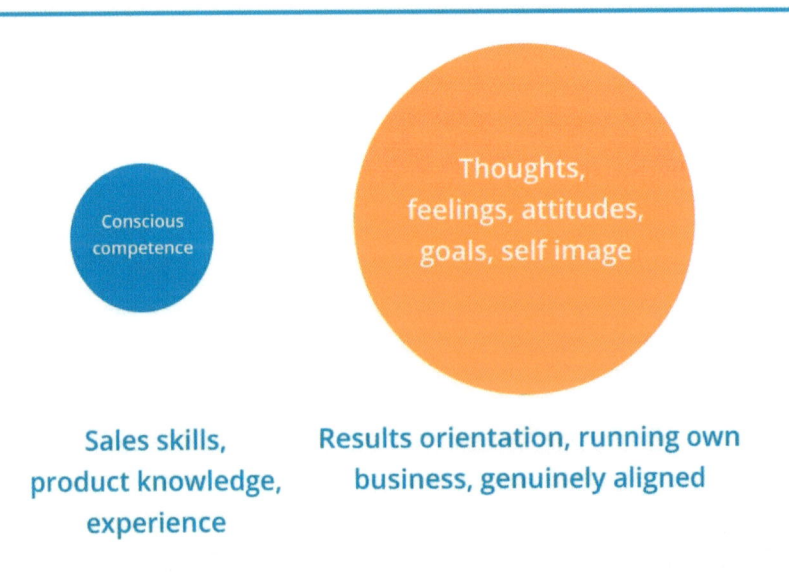

Conscious competence

Thoughts, feelings, attitudes, goals, self image

Sales skills, product knowledge, experience

Results orientation, running own business, genuinely aligned

Contrary to what most companies who think product and market knowledge are the key drivers of sales success ('ours is a very technical sell'), we find that the overall approach and attitude are usually four times as significant in ensuring success. Hence why you should test them!

Of course, without a rigorous process, it's quite difficult to pin down what 'good' looks like when recruiting for sales. In any sector or department, those who perform well at interview are generally those able to 'sell' themselves effectively face to face. But of course when you're dealing with experienced salespeople, they're more often than not going to do an excellent job of this. They still might not have quite the right skills and aptitudes to deliver the results you're intending to achieve within your growth plan, though.

It can be harder than you might think to make an objective decision from a CV, interview or even recommendations. There's just too much subjectivity involved. For example, we once assisted a client who was recruiting for a sales position in Scotland, and had three candidates attending an assessment day. In the morning, the (mainly Scottish) management team favoured two of the candidates (both Scottish), because they just seemed to 'click' more, and weren't sure about the third guy (who was from South East England).

We did personality profiles, as well as a series of exercises designed to test the various qualities we wanted, and the upshot was that eventually they chose the candidate initially at the bottom of their list, because he fulfilled the objective criteria much more successfully. Without the process of assessment, they would have made the wrong hire.

Similarly, we were tasked with providing an opinion on a candidate for a Head of Business Development role at a professional firm, and we were told he'd passed two telephone interviews with flying colours. He was City-based, very well connected in the right places, very professional, very personable, with a professional services background. So far so good. But I asked him a series of about eight questions during a 40-minute call, and it became apparent that he'd never been a Sales Manager, and didn't really have a grasp of what sales management really involves.

The client had already received some excellent references, and seemed keen, so I showed them a transcript of some of his answers, with a comparison example of a 'model' response (which was a mile away from what he'd said), and explained that I didn't have confidence in his ability to do the sales management job, and that I thought perhaps that the referees' view of what good looked like didn't marry up with the good we were looking for.

After taking a further reference from someone the investor knew well – the MD at one of the businesses the candidate had previously worked at – the feedback was that he was excellent at developing selling relationships, but there was a big gap in his knowledge regarding sales management. So rather than employ him for the full business development role initially intended, the client chose to employ him as the manager for the London area to see how he got on, while searching for a separate head of business development.

4.2 An Induction Process For Faster Performance

As well as using the right recruitment process to ensure new starts have the right innate preferences and abilities for the sales role in question, it's important to pin down the job description and have a strong induction process. This means every new employee can hit the ground running, and start with the best possible chance of success.

Also known as 'onboarding', employee induction should always include the basics of the company's operations and values, rules, conventions, processes, and 'housekeeping' for all staff. But in sales there's another specific set of information that's critical to success - and without it even the best salespeople and managers risk underperformance.

New starts need to know what the KPIs are and how they are used, as well as the key propositions and how to make best use of them in the field, as well as (for managers) how the right talent should be continually managed and nurtured. It's simply not enough to give them product knowledge and tell them to go off and sell.

I'd also recommend that anybody newly joining the sales department spends some time with each part of the business. It's a bit of an obvious HR thing, but generally speaking salespeople often don't get to understand how the rest of the company works. It's actually really important if you're going to go out there and sell to people. It's not that they need to be able to explain how the business works, but they do need the certainty that, when the customer eventually places business and it goes to this part of the organization, they can be sure it will deliver because they've seen it for themselves.

It's much more to do with giving them the confidence that then naturally comes across, than it is having the good knowledge of how the company operates, which the customer won't need to know.

For the quickest start, you also need to equip people with clear knowledge of performance expectations, and an idea of the basic tools they'll need to achieve that from day one. A clear job description will naturally be part of this, but you should also cover the 'how' of achieving the required results. Naturally everybody's approach is personal to them, but you can at least offer an idea of the set of inputs to the sales process that would be expected to deliver the outcome you're asking of them[7]. As time goes on a more individualized version can be developed.

This approach won't necessarily ensure success, but it will ensure that you get an early idea of whether a new start is capable of succeeding and if they are, then it will help them to do so. If they can't work to the plan, they're the wrong people, and if they are working to that plan it gives them confidence that they're getting off on the right foot and doing the right things and the results will follow.

We've found that many sales departments don't approach the induction process in this way. It doesn't mean their salespeople won't perform, but it does mean it'll likely take three times longer than it should do. Why wait all that time to improve revenue?

---

[7] See appendix for examples of useful working documents [GONOGO Assessment and Call Plan Template]

TIPS TO AVOID THE TRAPS

- Do the role descriptions set out attitudes not just skills/experience?
- Are the core skills tested *before hiring, by a sales professional rather than HR?*
- Are the core attitudes tested before hiring?
- Is the induction process at least a month long? Does it involve spending at least a day with all departments?
- Will new hires be taught how to sell for their new employer specifically?
- Are there core propositions set out to sell with, including a consultative selling-based question framework?

4.3 Summary

So, having read this book, and learned some of the secrets of our 3 Cs Methodology, you should now be in a position to:

- Quickly assess the quality of the sales management team in front of you
- Speedily ascertain whether or not the Information Memorandum contains all the information you need
- Rapidly evaluate whether a company's board can drive the required growth itself, or whether an outsourced specialist perspective would be beneficial

You have access to the tools and thinking that underpin the 3 Cs Model, which leads to bigger sales results and growth for your business:

Our Three 'C' methodology

Sales Result

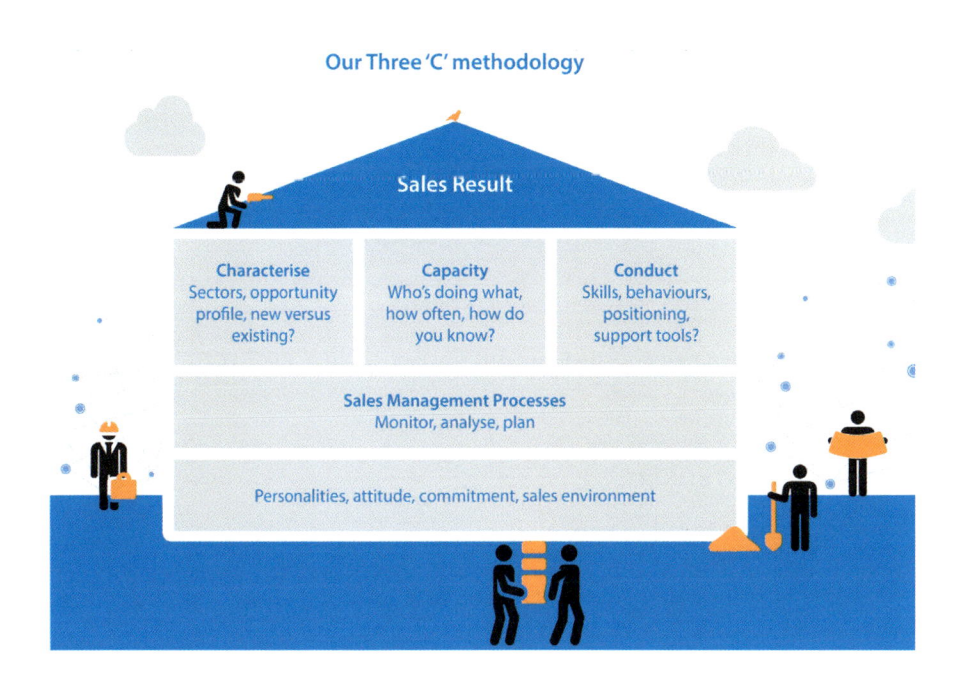

Characterise	Capacity	Conduct
Sectors, opportunity profile, new versus existing?	Who's doing what, how often, how do you know?	Skills, behaviours, positioning, support tools?

Sales Management Processes
Monitor, analyse, plan

Personalities, attitude, commitment, sales environment

Of course, we are ideally placed to be that outsourced perspective, as specialists in helping private equity backed businesses to reach their full potential, enhancing shareholder value through double-digit percentage growth for the revenue line prior to exit. Over the last 16 years, Sales Blueprint has carried out more than 200 projects for companies (both pre- and post-investment), across a wide variety of sectors, and we've worked for almost half of the UK mid-market private equity firms. Why do they choose us? Because our 3 Cs Methodology gets results, fast.

Thanks to our team's combined 60+ years' experience in B2B sales and marketing, we can deliver all the right outcomes to typically achieve a 25% increase in sales in year one, and create a basis for sustainable growth. These include:

- A clear, focused Sales & Marketing policy and direction
- Increased sales revenues
- Improved sold margins
- Sustainable levels of increased sales activity
- Improved accuracy of forecasting
- Improved retention and penetration of key accounts
- Improved market penetration
- Improved brand recognition

But, you might ask, do we practice what we preach? Of course we do. Which is why we have developed a profile of the type of business that represents the best fit for our services:

- A desire to achieve at least 10% growth, typically exceeding market growth rates
- Recognition of the importance of the sales function in achieving this
- Tangible appetite for change

- Primary route to market is via personal selling, either face-to-face or over the telephone
- UK-based sales operation
- Sales force of between two and 50 people

Of course, best practice is best practice, whatever the size of company or business sector, but we have found that companies that meet the above criteria benefit the most from our consultancy services, and enjoy superlative growth by following our recommendations. To find out more, please call 0161 374 4774, or visit www.salesblueprint.co.uk.

About Graeme Hall

With almost 30 years' experience in B2B sales, and a career that's brought him into contact with some of the world's top sales talent, Graeme set up Sales Blueprint in 2000, to help effect positive change in the top line of private equity backed businesses. He's known for his pragmatic, no-nonsense approach to sales operations consultancy, and his in-depth knowledge of the dynamics and structure of effective sales forces, as well as his ability to effect significant improvements in performance - with a singular focus on delivering results that meet clients' objectives and exceeding their expectations.

Appendices

Ideal Opportunity Profile

Initial enquiry screen	
Date created	**Monday, 10 May 10**
Company name	
Enquiry Number	

CRITERION	Comment	Score
Customer turnover (£) company or division	>£100m	4
Purchasing history (New equipment)	>3 years	0
Used Meltech before	Yes	2
Predicted project value (£)	<£50k	0
Location	Europe	0
Order placement timescale	>12 months	0
Reason for enquiry	Researching market	0
Technical risk	High	0
Potential for further work	None	0
TOTAL SCORE	UNLIKELY	6

The Basics of Sales Process and Activity Planning

- Establish the type of business you want to win, where to find it;
- Agree a method by which you can 'objectively' assess and qualify it;
- Establish how much brand new, new logo business you want versus new from existing;
- Assuming there is sufficient opportunity to satisfy your ambitions in your chosen markets, map the steps in the sale for each type of business you have, taking account of the likely differences in the process for new versus existing; Typical steps will be Qualification, Discovery (establishing key needs and wants, understanding timescales, decision-making process/people etc.), maybe Proof of Concept, Proposal, Negotiation, Closure;
- Within each section you will need to establish the activities that are necessary (for Discovery this could be 1st meeting, follow up meeting etc.) and how long you would expect each to take - how many meetings can you do in a day for example helps take easy account of the travelling time;

- You then need to guesstimate the dependencies from each stage to the next (assuming you don't already know of course!) - what percentage of opportunities in Discovery phase make it through to the next one for example?;
- Allied to the typical year one value of the typical/ideal opportunity, you can work out how many opportunities you need at the beginning of each process, to get one through to the end. Multiply this figure by the number of typical deals you need and you have the total number of opportunities of each type and the number of each type of activity the business will have to perform. You will also now know the total amount of time each deal will consume and therefore the total amount of business development time you will need as a whole.;
- You also need to take account of the elapsed time to get a typical opportunity all the way to close;
- If each business development person has a target to deliver, you can easily calculate the amount of time this will take, given the above.
- For each business development person (or part thereof for people who only do some of this) you should subtract the time spent on other tasks that don't include any of the activities in the sales process, from 221 days (365 minus

weekends) and make sure that the remaining figure is less than the time necessary to deliver their target!

- Either inside or outside of CRM, all activities should be recorded under the now settled headings and you can start to develop a 'dashboard' of 'upstream' indicators of on or off-target performance *before the order book is impacted.*

Key Differences Between Sales Directors and Sales Managers

Sales Manager	Sales Director
• Primarily tactical and operational • May have channel/line of business responsibility • Ensures resource is sufficient to deliver targets • Operates with no more than 6-8 direct reports • Creates and ensures delivery of activity levels • Delivers key targets through the sales resource • Monitors and sets targets • Identifies skills gaps • Field accompaniment visits • Coaches to close skill gaps • Supports key bids and relationships	• Strategic approach to overall company sales performance, now and in the future • Responsible for sales aspects of overall business plan and delivering overall number • May manage several Sales Managers • Often responsible for marketing direction and plan • If so may manage several Marketing Managers, who are charged with executing the marketing plans • Responsible for gathering key market intelligence • Creates overall sales policy with respect to products, prices, customer mix etc.

- May manage some accounts depending on business size
- Implements commission scheme
- Helps influence product/service development
- Helps influence customer service levels
- Monitors and implements expense scheme and other related admin
- Ensures adherence with general sales related company procedures

- Ensures sales policy remains in line with overall company objectives and market intelligence
- Creates 'go to market' strategy and develops necessary resource
- Develops strategic partnerships
- Participates in Board discussion and reporting
- Develops overall sales methodologies
- Develops sales process
- Develops necessary sales systems
- Develops sales related company procedures
- Sets parameters for overall quality of necessary resource, core competences, skills etc
- Sets out policy for remuneration across the whole sales team

In-Call Assessment Forms

Salesman	Date	Client
Objectives of Call		
Preparation Work		
Sales Figures		
Sales Tools		

In Call Performance	Rating 1 - 5	Comments
Introduction / Setting the Agenda		
Questioning Techniques		
Drill Down		
Listen to Learn		
Identifying Opportunities		
Selling in of Objectives		
Handling Objections		

Promotion of Additional Products / Services		
Agenda set for next meeting		
Action Required from Minutes		
Summary of Call		
Remarks		
Overall Assessment Rating		

Details	Score
No use or understanding of sales structure / techniques - training imperative	1
Partial use and understanding of sales structure / techniques - improvement needed	2
Good use and understanding of sales structure / techniques - develop weak areas	3
Consistent use and understanding of sales structure / techniques - refresh skills	4
Excellent use and understanding of sales structure / techniques - maintain quality	5

GONOGO Assessment

> Mandatory cells without which we can not realistically forecast

Company name		Date created	
Enquiry Number		Latest update	

	CRITERION	Answer	Score	Comments	Actions
Got Money	Are our costs within the customer's budget?	Yes	3	What is it?	
	Have they confirmed this?	Yes	5	When? Evidence?	
	When do they wish to order?		0	How do you know?	
	Do we know whose budget it is?	Yes	5	Whose?	
Our solution	Has the client expressed a preference for our solution?	Yes	3	When?	

	CRITERION	Answer	Score	Comments	Actions
	Have we any specific advantages?	Yes	3	What are they?	
	Are our advantages central to the customer's perception of their problems?	Yes	3	How do you know?	
	Have we a good track record with the customer?	Yes	3		
	Have we received a strong recommendation from someone the customer respects?	Yes	5	Who?	
Needs	Do we <u>really</u> understand the customer's needs and wants?	Yes	5	What are they in detail?	

107

	CRITERION	Answer	Score	Comments	Actions
	Has the customer <u>confirmed</u> that we understand them correctly?	Yes	5	When? Evidence?	
	Do we understand the needs and wants of <u>all</u> the people in the decision-making-process?	Yes	5	Who are they? What do they want?	
	Are the needs realistic?	Yes	3	How do you know?	
One decision-maker	Do the decision-makers know they have a decision to make?	Yes	5	When does it have to be taken by?	
	Are we talking to <u>all</u> of the decision-makers	Yes	5	Who are they?	

	CRITERION	Answer	Score	Comments	Actions
	Do we have credibility with the Exec level?	Yes	5	With whom exactly?	
	Is our proposal still current?	Yes	5	How old is it?	
	Does the customer express a bias towards us?	Yes	5	How?	
Got resources?	Can we realistically meet all of the customer's needs and wants?	Yes	3	Show me the plan	
	Can we perform within the time scales that the customer is happy with?	Yes	5	Have Ops confirmed this?	
	Is the contract within our current capability?	Yes	3	Have Ops confirmed this?	

	CRITERION	Answer	Score	Comments	Actions
	Have we agreed an implement-ation plan with the customer?	Yes	5	Show me the plan	
Only bidder	Are we the only bidder?	Yes	10	How do we know?	
	Is there another bidder?	Yes	5	Who is it?	
	Is there more than one other bidder?	Yes	3	Who are they?	
	Are there more than two other bidders?	Yes	2	Who are they?	
	Does the competition have any unique advantages in the eyes of the customer?	Yes	0	What are they in detail?	

CRITERION	Answer	Score	Comments	Actions
Are the competition dealing at a higher level than us?	No	3	How do you know?	
Do the competition have a strong track record with the customer?	No	3		
TOTAL SCORE	**0**	**110**		

Call Plan Template

Prospect/Customer:	Meeting with:	Date/time of meeting:

- *What would be a good outcome of your meeting?*
- *What would be a great step forward and progress towards increasing your business with this client?*

1.	2.
3.	4.

Valid business reason for the meeting *(from the PROSPECT/CUSTOMER'S point of view)*

What information can you gather BEFORE the meeting? (What sources of information will you use?)

What information will you try to get during the appointment? *(Ask yourself what information do you require in order to establish a firm foundation onto which to build your later proposals?)*

QUESTIONS: *Your control of the appointment should be based on the O.P.E.N.U.P. framework. Start them with "Who", "What", "Where", "When" and "How". Be careful how you construct them. Make it a conversation and not an interrogation. Remember not to make any assumptions. NO GUESSING! Write down the specific questions you will ask:*

WHAT NEEDS TO BE CONFIRMED? (Duration of meeting: his/her objectives)	**WHAT NEW INFORMATION DO YOU NEED?**
WHAT GENERAL OPEN QUESTIONS WILL YOU ASK?	**WHAT COMMITMENT QUESTIONS? TIMESCALES/BUDGET/DMU?**

HOW WILL YOU OPEN THE MEETING? (*This should demonstrate to the prospect customer that you have researched their business and have a basic understanding of their issues and high-level view of what they do. This should also set the scene that you want to investigate their needs at a high level initially before you settle down to discuss any specific deals and requirements) A short clear statement which explains why this customer should listen to you ('Elevator Pitch'). Should also include an OPEN QUESTION at the end in order to get this customer talking about his/her business needs*)

WHAT IS YOUR BEST ACTION AS A RESULT OF THIS MEETING?	**WHAT IS THE MINIMUM YOU WILL ACCEPT?**
WHAT OBJECTIONS MIGHT YOU ENCOUNTER?	**HOW WILL YOU RESPOND?** (*Give (compelling) examples with client references*)

REMEMBER THE USE OF SILENCE – *Listen to* **your prospect/customer**

Your Prospect/Customer's Decision Making Unit

You need to work out who will play what role in your customers buying process and treat them appropriately. So let's look at **D**ecision **M**aking **U**nits and how they are made up.

User: Generally make use of the service/product, low influence but shouldn't be ignored
Screen: Can't ultimately say YES but can say a definite NO
Sign Off: Have formal authority to place orders, select suppliers and release funds
Champion: Someone within the target organisation who will sell for you when you aren't there
Navigator: Might be outside the target organisation but helps with the sale process/information flow

People can and do play different and more than one role in the same opportunity.

For this opportunity fill in who are the various players in the Customer's DMU:

Name of Person	Role Played in DMU

Appointment Review

On a scale of 1 = Poor and 10 = Excellent:	1	2	3	4	5	6	7	8	9	10
How prepared were you?										
Was your research relevant to the meeting?										
How good were your opening questions?										
Did you control the meeting with questions?										
Did you get the information you needed?										
To what extent did you make them think?										
Were you able to directly link the advantages of your products/services to your client's objectives?										
How valuable are the opportunities that you uncovered?										
Did both parties walk away with actions from the meeting?										

Specifically what would you do differently next time?

Printed in Great Britain
by Amazon